Home Decoration and Furnishing

The New Look of Chinese Homes

LONG RIVER PRESS
San Francisco

English edition © 2005 by Shanghai Press and Publishing Development Company

Chinese edition © 2004 by Shanghai Lexicographical Publishing House

All rights reserved. Unauthorized reproduction, in any manner, is prohibited.

This book is edited and designed by the Editorial Committee of *Cultural China* series.

Managing Editors: Naiqing Xu, Youbu Wang, Ying Wu

Project Designer (Chinese): Xiaobo Shangguan

Executive Editor: Ying Wu

Interior and Cover Design: Yinchang Yuan, Jing Li

Photographs by Zhicheng Chai, Shiwang Bao, Zhan Jin, etc.

Text by Yaxian Wu, Dongmei Zhu, Ren Zhong

Translation by Sylvia Yu, Julian Chen, and Christopher Malone

ISBN 1-59265-061-9

Library of Congress Control Number: 2005934901

Published by

Long River Press

360 Swift Ave., Suite 48

South San Francisco, CA 94080

USA

and

Shanghai Press and Publishing Development Company

1110 Huaihai Middle Road, Donghu Villa F, Shanghai, China (200031)

Computer typeset by Yuan Yinchang Design Studio, Shanghai

Printed in China by Shanghai Donnelley Printing Co. Ltd.

1   2   3   4   5   6   7   8   9   10

Foreword

China and the West differ greatly in culture and traditions, especially in the field of architecture and decoration. However, in many individual cases of successful design, we find a convergence of Chinese and Western elements. Furniture from the Ming and Qing dynasties, ceramics, textiles, calligraphy, jadeware, bamboo sculptures, Chinese knots - these unique elements have been cleverly incorporated in the design of the modern living space. This new wave of Chinoiserie is marked by extremely simple modern design rooted in profound Chinese philosophy. It features smooth, simple outlines, refined, well-thought out structures, perfect proportions and surprising versatility.

It has become a trend to use elements from traditional Chinese architecture and decoration to light up today's home. The trend embodies modern people's appreciation of traditional Chinese aesthetic concepts and philosophy of life.

Through this collection of photographs, we aim to present a glimpse of the oriental ethos of balance and harmony behind the totem patterns and the splendid and meticulous woodcarvings. This is the unique charm of Chinoiserie.

Elements of Chinoiserie

1. Ming and Qing style furniture: Ming and Qing furniture, especially Ming furniture, features simple lines and shapes and uses quality materials. Even if one cannot own genuine antiques, hand-made modern replicas using traditional techniques may be used to achieve the Chinoiserie feel at home.

2. Country style: The use of vine, wood, bamboo and other natural and rough looking materials as design element imparts a strong Chinese character. Bamboo curtains, bamboo-strip mats, wooden stools and rattan chairs can create a simple and natural atmosphere.

3. Home textiles: Chinese silk and embroidery are integral decorative elements in the creation of Chinoiserie. Pendant ornaments, cushions, bedding, screen partitions, tablecloths and napkins can all be used for decoration and are collectibles in their own right. Hand-woven carpets and tapestries of Chinese calligraphy and paintings are also valuable works of art.

4. Display items: Rooms displaying Chinoiserie items immediately feel very Chinese. There are several categories of display items, namely ceramics, bronze, woodenware and lacquerware and so on. In addition, Buddhist statues, calligraphy and paintings with auspicious connotations, and lanterns can likewise enhance Chinoiserie.

Chinoiserie in Larger Spaces

Large black and red patterns set off the exquisite display items and the meticulous decorative details and greatly enhance the appeal of the entire open space.

1. The bronze door of the storage room is the most important symbol of Chinese architecture and is very engaging visually.

2. A large expanse of brick wall, an ancient Chinese window lattice, a colorful low cabinet, and the ceramic piece displayed on the cabinet are all characteristic of Chinoiserie.

Home Decoration and Furnishing

The ingenious lighting adds great interest to the traditional Chinese painting on the wall and the intricately carved screen partition.

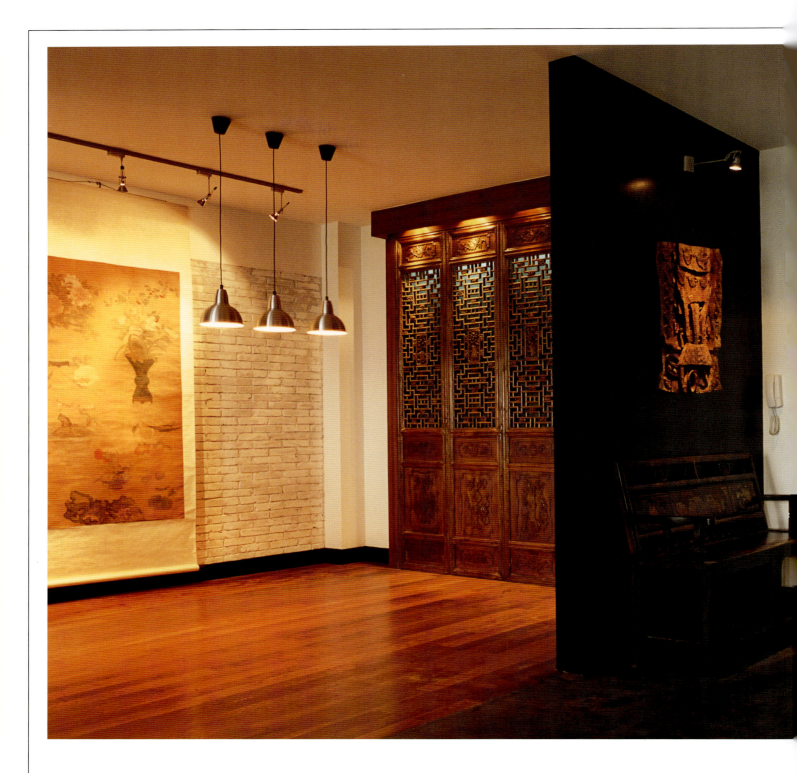

A piece of black wood hung with a Chinoiserie ornament doubles as the partition at the entrance. Besides serving as a screen, it brings an added sense of discretion to the whole room.

A distinct play of colors marks this bathroom. Black, red and white match and complement each other.

The Classic Chinese window lattice is a commonly used element. On the back shelf, the owner displays the antiques in his collection to strong decorative effect.

Home Decoration and Furnishing

014

Modernity and a Return to the Past
In designer Simon's 400-square-meter home, many traditional Chinese elements have been brought up to date. They integrate well with the modern décor, and are rich in imagination.

Left: It is a wonderful idea to use these ancient windows and doors, carved from wood and dismantled from ancient houses, to line the whole wall. Right: There is a striking decorative effect in using traditional Chinese symbols of auspiciousness on the doors.

A camphorwood trunk once commonplace in ordinary Chinese households is used here as the base for a blue and white porcelain washbasin. Two Chinese elements are thus combined immaculately.

The modern industrial creation of the Hi-Fi blends well with its simple and unadorned surrounding. The ancient brick wall functions as a spatial transition between the two worlds.

The ingenious use of bamboo conveys a sense of nature even in a very modern space.

The New Look of Chinese Homes

Home Decoration and Furnishing 022

A Frenchman's Chinese House
The Frenchman has a fond passion for the Chinese style. Ming-style round-backed armchairs share the space with Miesian chairs. A remodeled big Chinese cabinet now stores French wines. The owner's awesome imaginative and creative powers are very much in evidence.

The New Look of Chinese Homes

Left: Miesian chairs are placed alongside traditional Chinese furniture. Modern electronic appliances such as the TV and video player are hidden discreetly in a Chinese cabinet, which was originally designed to store quilts. Traditional furniture is put to novel use.

1. The brightly colored brocade cushions on the round-backed armchair and deckchair light up the room.
2. Traditional wooden carved partitions are used to decorate this modern false ceiling to create a unique atmosphere.

1

2

A Chinese carved wooden partition divides the room.

The New Look of Chinese Homes

The owner must have expended great efforts in scouting out these pieces of furniture. The contrast in colors between the furniture and walls is striking.

Home Decoration and Furnishing

Beyond Furnishings
The substantial number of paintings, reliefs and pieces of antique furniture and the walls, false ceilings and lighting designed to set them off combine to bring this unit alive.

A large wooden relief is set off by a black background, an idea showing extraordinary artistic flair.

An ancient wood partition separates the space. The exquisitely carved low cabinet stands in stark contrast with the white wall, projecting vivid visual effect.

Gray brick flooring, red walls, and inventive lighting combine to create a pleasant effect. In a very unique approach, the gray brick is applied to the wall of the glass shower room. An old-fashioned wooden armchair stands nearby. It is both functional and decorative.

Neo-Rural Style

The interior design of this household is inspired by rural Chinoiserie. The furniture adopts a distinct rural vernacular that has been revitalized for modern living. Clearly the owner has a very original mind.

The pale yellow wall echoes the simple and plain furniture.

1. A two-drawer, two-door carved cabinet.
2. A side cabinet and two chairs in the dining room.
3. This long, low cabinet used to be an altar table in a Shanxi temple.
4. This big six-part cabinet from Shanxi, made during the late Ming or early Qing Dynasty, now sits in the living room. The painting above it comes from Anhui.

Two chairs from the Ming dynasty with the top of the back shaped like a mandarin's hat. The carved cabinet comes from the early Qing dynasty.

1. A big, red-lacquer, gilded cabinet from a rich Shanxi household. The working desk in front was designed by the owner himself and represents a perfect combination of the old and the modern.

2. A pair of hand-painted Mongolian trunks are now used by the owner to store magazines.

3. A typical Ming big-small cabinet pair from the southern China. Placed on top are printing boards and cake moulds.

1. Living room – a Qing washstand from Shandong, and round-backed armchair for women from the late Qing dynasty.
2. Living room – this carved cabinet with three drawers and two storage spaces comes from a wealthy and influential Shanxi household; it used to be an altar table.
3. The brick reliefs on the wall come from a screen wall in Shanxi.
4. Study – a bean curd rack from a rich household becomes a tea table for the new owner.

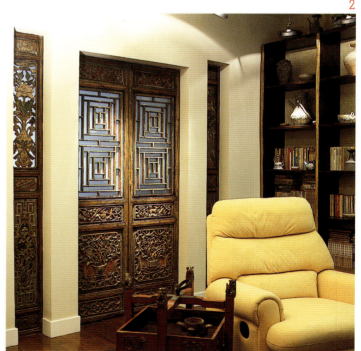

1. Kitchen – a wooden cabinet with a glazed back.
2. Brick reliefs from a screen wall in Shanxi are embedded on the walls.
3. Framing the arch door is a wood relief.

1

2

3

Wood from Gansu is combined with modern materials such as stainless steel and glass.

1. A couch with railing from a rich Shanxi household; it is more than 300 years old. The combination of red and yellow is outstanding; the colors of the walls and cushions match well.
2. A Mongolian *kang* (a heatable brick bed) table in the front, and a carved Shanxi Buddhist cabinet at the back.
3. A *kang* cabinet for storing quilts melds both Shanxi and Mongolia styles. When railing and cushions are added, it can be used as a sofa.
4. A 3-drawer tableware shelf is now a TV stand.

1

2

3

4

On the balcony – this Shanxi bench used to be placed at the entrance of a temple. With red and yellow cushions, it looks simple and primitive and yet brims with life.

A Love for Antiques

On the exquisitely carved Malaysian cabinet (used for storing shoes) on the left side of the entrance stands an old wooden Buddhist statue. Two wood sculptures of the elephant from Thailand are at the Buddha's feet. An old *kang* cabinet on the right side of the entrance is at once ornamental and functional (as a chair).

The ancient tall red lacquer cabinet painted in gold lines, standing in the corner of the sitting-room, came from Shanxi Province; and the low three-door cabinet came from Beijing.

Home Decoration and Furnishing

Home Decoration and Furnishing 048

An Encounter with the South

This ordinary house, found in a picturesque old town south of the Yangtze River, is refined in its interior furnishings. Behind the solid wooden door, there is a long corridor paved with gray bricks. The basket lantern placed in front of the Chinese

window lattice exudes a unique charm. However, the most striking aspect of the room is a western style dining table made out of two big beams from Suzhou. Beside the table, small, exquisite bamboo chairs would be put At the same time, modern comfort and leisure is never missing in this rural household.

The air-conditioner is hidden behind a specially made wooden frame, to avoid ruining the overall atmosphere.

The entire back section of the second floor of the building has been remodeled and revitalized.

1. The gray brick and white lime joints are intentionally left bare in order to create a natural and unsophisticated ambience.

2. The clever combination of a small bamboo chair and a computer.

3. The Chinoiserie wooden frame in the corridor creates a natural space.

1

2

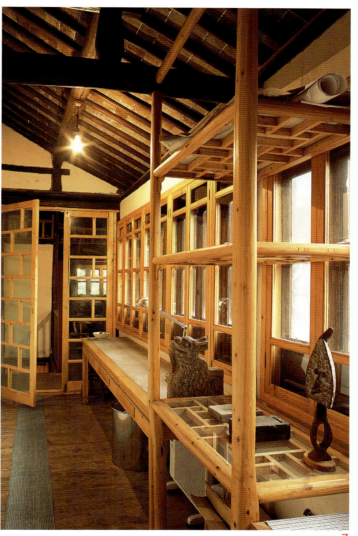

3

1. The bathroom is hidden behind a carved wooden door. Wood and stone mix naturally in this small space.

2. Carved wooden window lattices combine with a streamline cut wood block to form a bathroom counter.

3. At the corner of the bathroom, one can catch a glimpse of the springtime courtyard through a window. The cobblestone-paved floor brings one even closer to nature.

4. There is a large amount of wood in the bathroom, with well-appointed Chinoiserie details.

1. A Chinese fireplace designed by Mr. Hu himself. Laid with bricks, it is very practical and can be found in every room.
2. A square dining table is set beside the kitchen stove. The tablecloth features simple rural color combination and design pattern.
3. The kitchen stove commonly seen in households south of the Yangtze River.
4. A piece of cotton covers a stone stool beside an architectural column, affording one a place to sit on. A modern abstract painting on the wall makes for an interesting contrast to the handicraft below.

1

2

3

4

Home Decoration and Furnishing

054

East Meets West

The combination of red bricks, white porcelain, mirrors, and a Shanxi cabinet is a perfect example of East meeting West – of an oasis of artlessness in our modern times.

In the open bathroom, an old cabinet is refashioned into a bathroom counter. The

drawers have been modified to allow the passage of waterpipes. The cast-iron wall lamp between the two mirrors is Spanish in style.
A freestanding bath with dedicated spotlights.
The color of the bamboo curtains echoes the dominant color tones of the room.

Home Decoration and Furnishing

1. An integrated western-style kitchen and dining room.
2. The modern kitchen cabinets contrast intriguingly with the rural dining table and small wooden stools.
Right: The highlight of the living room is an ancient gold-traced altar table which used to stand in a temple. Handed down from the Qing dynasty, it is now the mantelpiece of the newly constructed fireplace. To add depth to the chamber, a half-length, thick brick wall has been laid, and the exposed bricks are then painted white.

1

2

A Spanish cast-iron chandelier shares the space with a Chinese wooden palace lantern.

The Charm of Soft Decoration

Soft decoration cannot be overlooked in a refined household. Well-conceived soft decoration can often have a transforming effect.

Left: This Dripping Guanyin shaped plant is over 2 meters tall. It is the liveliest element of the living room and brings vitality to the entire room.

Right: An old camphorwood trunk, a Buddha's head, pieces of embroidery, and a large splash-ink painting of a lotus all show the remarkable fine taste of the owner.

Tradition and Modernity

The major features of this 280-square-meter villa lie in the melding of modern concepts with a more traditional style. The designer does not simply deploy the Chinese elements for their sake; he relies on the interplay of colors, materials and lighting to give his own rendition of Chinoiserie.

Left: The back wall is laid with tiles. In front of the wall is an exquisite lacquer cabinet, on the top of which is a blue and white porcelain. This corner of the room has thus acquired a rather distinct character. The gray stone flooring embedded in white sand is yet another inspired touch.

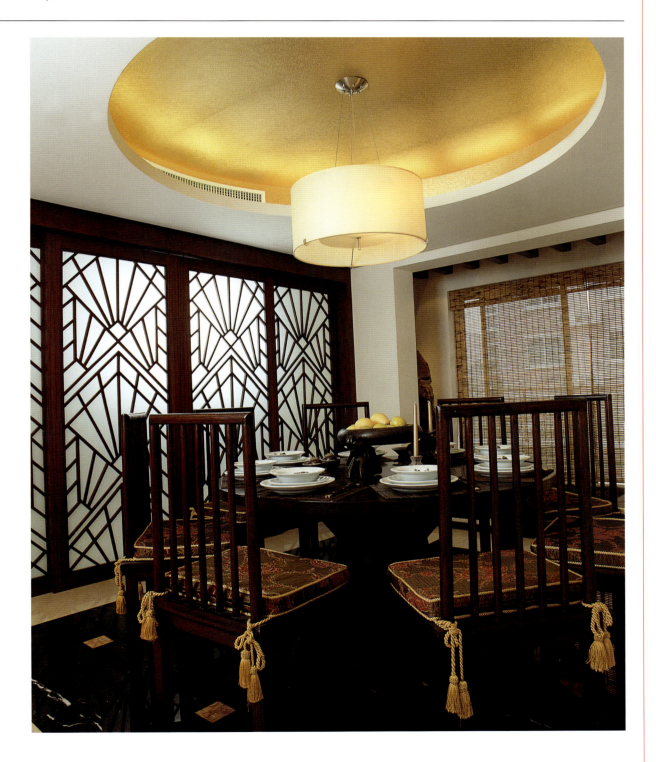

Words from "Ode to Chibi", a famous ancient essay, are rendered in calligraphic relief on the wall. From this, one gathers that this must be a highly cultivated household. The yellow light, curtains, sofas, and colors of the side frame are all well conceived, making the room an oasis of tranquility and harmony.

Home Decoration and Furnishing

Build One's Own Love Nest

The big red bed, bedding, and low cabinet on the side set the main color tone of the room. Purple and bright yellow walls further enhance the atmosphere.

The New Look of Chinese Homes

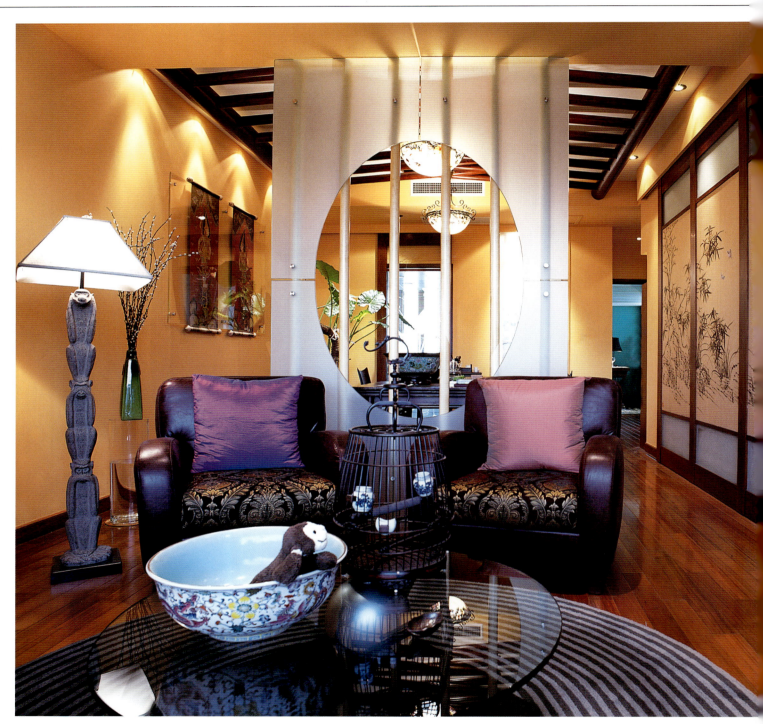

This design, from the shapes (spatial geometry with circles and straight lines) to the large expanses of colors (bright yellow, tender green and purple) is very modern. Chinese details add another dimension to the room. It is worth noting that lighting is especially important to this kind of design.

Bamboo curtains, a bird-cage and flowers conspire to create a leisurely and vivacious ambience.

The lighting corresponds to the large expanse of bright yellow on the wall, creating a lively and refreshing feel.

It must be pleasurable to dine in this bright and delightful dining-room.

From the darkish pink color of the study one can feel the cheerful disposition of the female owner.

Home Decoration and Furnishing

One can see the green of the bedroom from the dining room. Changing colors trigger a visual leap.

The green of the bedroom brings one closer to nature, while the calligraphy on the wall adds poetry to the room.

Home Decoration and Furnishing

All in the Space of 80 Square Meters
One doesn't feel cramped in this well-conceived and cleverly-furnished apartment. The furniture and ornamental items are traditionally Chinese.

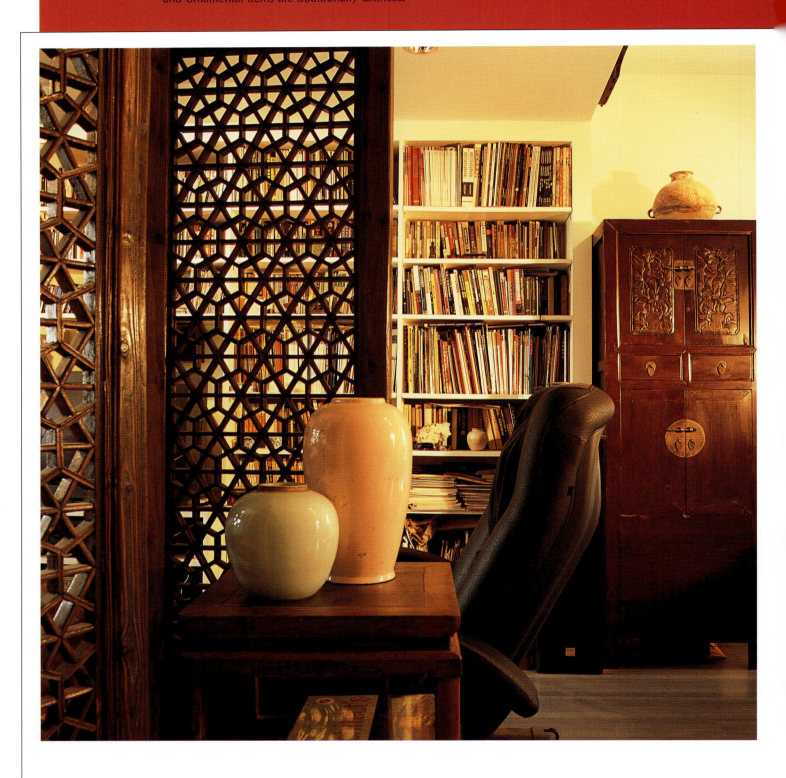

Strike Out on One's Own

This well-appointed western villa has a look that is at once steeped in Chinese literary tradition and contemporary in its fresh and cheerful ambience. While the lines are angular, they are never harsh, helped by incorporation of Chinese elements and the use of warm lighting and natural materials.

Home Decoration and Furnishing

The Flavor of the Ming and Qing Dynasties
This house of a young Chinese artist boasts a veritable cornucopia of Chinese traditional ethnic and religious artifacts.

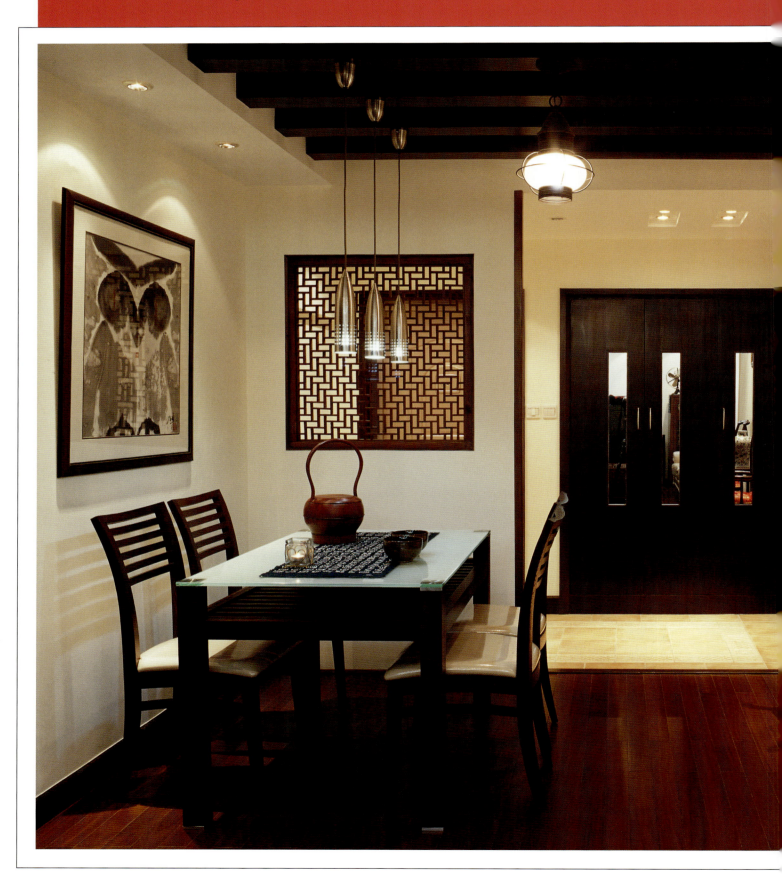

The New Look of Chinese Homes

The household displays and collected items often betray the aesthetic and artistic sensibility of the individual. In this case, we might wonder if they also have inspired and shaped the creations of the artist.

Home Decoration and Furnishing

To One's Heart's Content

The way one's home is decorated and furnished usually reflects the owner's character. An old trunk is used as a tea table, old doors with knockers as a large tabletop, and low teapoy as a stool etc. Use your imagination and follow your own way.

The wood latticed box-shaped lamp is also decorative.

Home Decoration and Furnishing

1. Goldfish in flowing water is a representative Chinese element. A white marble flower-pot is creatively used as the fishbowl.
2. Who would have thought that this door could be dismantled and used as a tabletop?

1

2

3

Traditionally Chinese are the bowls, plates, spoons, chopsticks and a teapot on the table, which is set in the western way.

The antiques and ornamental pieces are artistically displayed.

The owner is fond of large old furniture.

An ancient doorframe coupled with the simple bedroom decoration makes the room magnificent.

Peace and Harmony

Beautiful old Chinese furniture and wood carvings are tastefully incorporated in the design of this modern living space.

Home Decoration and Furnishing   110

A New Wave of Chinoiserie
The layout of this modern apartment has been adjusted to maximize functionality even as traditional motifs and details are discreetly introduced without seeming to suffocate the space.

The extensive use of sandalwood adds weight and a nostalgic touch to an apartment that is resolutely modern in design.

The Embrace of Mother Nature
Fine scenery through the large windows is decorative as Chinese paintings.

The Beauty of Softness
Flowers, fabrics and goldfish all contribute to perfect softness.

The predominance of fabrics, Chinese-character-inspired decorations and simple furnishings give the rooms an uncluttered look. The space is partitioned by lattice screens to add both privacy and depth and anchored by western sofas, which echo the many Chinese decorative details of the apartment.

Home Decoration and Furnishing

In the decoration and furnishing of this villa, fine points of Western art is interwoven with traditional Chinese style.

The New Look of Chinese Homes

Home in an Old Small Town
The new house is luxuriously furnished and decorated.

The basement is used as a home cinema. There are four small square stools under the table.

2. This unique partition at the entrance of a household is fronted with two Buddhist statues on cobblestones, conveying a mystic Buddhist presence.

Home Decoration and Furnishing

Individualities
Each and every home has its own individualities, betraying the likes and dislikes of the owner.

The New Look of Chinese Homes

Home Decoration and Furnishing

Home Decoration and Furnishing

The Shangri-la Art Commune

This house is in the Shangri-la Art Commune, which is located in the Caoyang District of Beijing.

The New Look of Chinese Homes

1. The front hall has a fishpond.
2. These objects are made by the artist living in the house.

Simple and Natural Appeal

This is the home of Mr. Gong Yi, a player of the Chinese zither. The instruments he has collected decorate the wall.

The New Look of Chinese Homes

A Well-Kept Old House
This beautiful old house was built in 1928. It has just been renovated and tastefully furnished.

147 The New Look of Chinese Homes

Right: The bedside lamps are old hand-carried palace lanterns.

Plants usually liven up a room full of antiques and other old things. Even a small vase of water plant can play an important role.

The New Look of Chinese Homes

Nostalgia for the Past

A modern kitchen and its cooking utensils are in harmony with the simple, primitive wooden stools and countertop. The exquisite chandelier and rough walls achieve an interesting balance.

The New Look of Chinese Homes

Home Decoration and Furnishing

The red and black tones in the bedroom are at once cheerful and discreet.

The combination of black and red is the most important color combination in Chinoiserie.

Two semi-circular arch doors add another layer of space to the common area. The pale green sofas and the plants in the background create a sense of vitality and nature.

A private meditation space of the male owner.

The sloping ceiling in the bathroom is very romantic. The bath near the window was converted from a beer barrel. One feels like having a sunbath and luxuriating in the sublime comfort. The washbasin (right) is made out of an old horse-feed bucket, evoking nostalgic thoughts.

Home Decoration and Furnishing

The terra cotta soldier at the entrance inevitably uncorks surprise and admiration from a visitor.

Let Nature Take Its Course
People living in this house are very fond of flowers and trees.

Man-Made Beauty

The length of the long table is just right, and so are the width and height of the beautifully carved "doors" decorating the wall.

175 The New Look of Chinese Homes

1. The kitchen is behind the door.
2. Old classical furniture stands gracefully on the gray brick floor.

A pierced, carved window frame is set in the wall and used as the partition at the entrance. This creates a scene of exceptional vividness and beauty.

Home Decoration and Furnishing

Rockery, bamboos, flowers and brick walls, all combine to create a scene of liveliness and beauty.

Home Decoration and Furnishing

Elaborately Carved Furniture

In this house, which is a retreat from the pressures of modern civilization, there are many pieces of elaborately carved furniture.

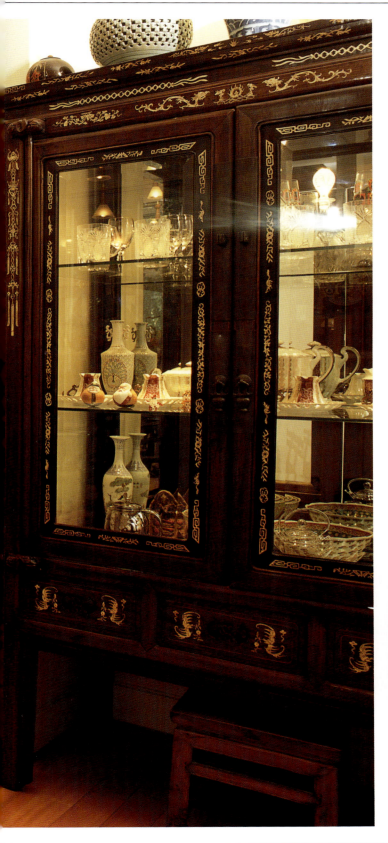

The New Look of Chinese Homes

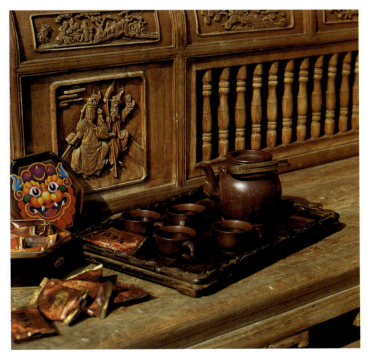

A Luxuriously Furnished House

Mahogany tables, chairs and cabinets, bonsai, Chinese paintings and blue-and-white porcelain, all combine to impart a strong Chinese character.

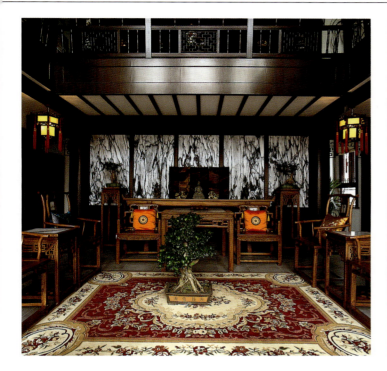